Remembering Farley

Other For Better or For Worse® Books

It's the Thought That Counts . . . Fifteenth Anniversary Collection
For Better or For Worse: The 10th Anniversary Collection
Starting from Scratch
"There Goes My Baby!"
Things Are Looking Up . . .
What, Me Pregnant?
If This Is a Lecture, How Long Will It Be?
Pushing 40
It's All Downhill From Here
Keep the Home Fries Burning
The Last Straw
Just One More Hug
"It Must Be Nice to Be Little"
Is This "One of Those Days," Daddy?
I've Got the One-More-Washload Blues . . .

A *For Better or For Worse*® Special Edition

Remembering Farley

A Tribute to the Life of Our Favorite Cartoon Dog

by Lynn Johnston

Andrews and McMeel
A Universal Press Syndicate Company
Kansas City

ISBN: 0-8362-1309-2

Library of Congress Catalog Card Number: 95-83104

First Printing, February 1996
Second Printing, December 1996

*B*ecause so many people requested a "Farley" retrospective, we have put together this collection and have included a few quotes from the many letters we have received.

DADDY, DADDY! - MRS BAIRD'S SHEEPDOG HAD PUPPIES AN' SHE SAYS WE CAN SEE THEM - WILL YOU COME? PLEASE?

HONEST, HONEY... WE'RE JUST GOING OVER TO LOOK!

OK...BUT IF YOU COME BACK WITH ONE... I QUIT!

JOHN AND MIKE HAVE BEEN LOOKING AT THOSE PUPPIES FOR OVER AN HOUR!

...THINK I'LL GO SEE WHAT'S KEEPING THEM.

.. THIS IS A TRAP, ISN'T IT.

HE'S A RUNT, YOU SEE... WE COULDN'T SELL HIM AND I'D HATE TO PUT HIM DOWN.

THE POOR LITTLE THING HAS BEEN REJECTED. HE'D NEED WARMTH AND LOVE TO SURVIVE!

GIVE ME ANOTHER SHOT AT HER MOTHER INSTINCTS AND YOU'VE GOT A DOG!

7

One rainy day, my son Patrick came home with a sheltie puppy he got from a friend at school. Like Elly, I didn't want the added responsibility of owning a dog. My objections were overruled by my family, and Tika moved in. Now, six years and many happy adventures later, she is my best friend and constant companion, and I wouldn't trade her for anything in the world!

Sharon Mason, Toronto, Canada

MICHAEL, I KNOW YOU LOVE FARLEY, BUT YOU'RE LOVING HIM TOO MUCH!

HOW WOULD YOU FEEL IF SOMEONE HUGE PICKED YOU UP AND SQUEEZED THE BREATH OUT OF YOU?

LET'S SEE... HOW WOULD I FEEL...

LIKE IT WAS MY BIRTHDAY AN' AUNT DOREEN WAS HERE?

HELLO?—YES... MAY I SPEAK TO THE VET, PLEASE?

DR. SCHELL.. I WAS WONDERING HOW LONG IT WOULD BE BEFORE WE COULD FEED OUR PUPPY TABLE SCRAPS.

REALLY?

YOU MEAN I'LL BE FINISHING THE KIDS' LEFTOVERS FOR ANOTHER SIX MONTHS?

• DISTRACTING YOUR PUPPY FROM UNWANTED BEHAVIOR
• PAPER TRAINING
• INTRODUCING THE LEASH...

DOG TRAINING

• GROOMING
• OBEDIENCE TRAINING FOR THE YOUNG DOG...

DOG TRAINING

BUT FIRST LET'S MAKE SURE HE SURVIVES CARE AND FEEDING!

DOG TRAINING

A puppy is more worth than it's trouble!

Mark Latimer,
Pueblo, Colo.

GRRRR!

SHRIEK

MOM! COME QUICK! — FARLEY'S GOT LIZZIE'S BUNNY!

HE'S SAVED!

MOM WILL FIX HIM, LIZZIE...

—SHE'S SUPER MOM!

...AND MOMENTS AGO I WAS JUST A MILD-MANNERED HOUSEWIFE.

MY DAD'S BEEN TAKIN' OUR DOG TO OBEDIENCE SCHOOL.

WHEN HE YELLS HEEL, FARLEY HEELS, WHEN HE YELLS SIT, FARLEY SITS...

AN' WHEN HE YELLS COME HE COMES — RIGHT?

SNAP

NOPE. WHEN HE YELLS FOOD HE COMES.

HI, MOM! — DON'T YOU JUST LOVE SPRING?

LOOK, IT'S NOT THAT I DON'T APPRECIATE FANCY DISHES!

I LIKE SIMPLE FOOD, THAT'S ALL!

I COULD PROBABLY EAT THE SAME THING EVERY DAY!

SURELY THERE ARE OTHERS LIKE ME!

MUNCH. MUNCH

15

17

Our dog, Frank, eats everything. He eats our cat's food and anything else he finds on the floor. One time we had to take him to the vet because he ate a plastic doll, a key chain (without the keys), and a long piece of string. I don't know if he's always hungry or if he just likes to eat.

David Steiner (age 11), Chicago, Ill.

21

24

My first dog was a sheepdog combination. His name was Wellington, and he was a great dog. Only growled once in his life, and that was at an intruder in my bedroom. Only bit once in his life, the same intruder. The police loved putting that in their report.

Maggie Rosenthal,
Jamaica Plain, Mass.

31

*L*et sleeping dogs lie. . . . And they'll usually choose a doorway.

Ruth Kennedy, North Vancouver, B.C.

In the Lap of Luxury (A Rare Hotel!)

The animals who come to stay with us are our guests. We set down the rules and we ease their fears by communicating with words, with feelings, and sometimes, massage.

At night they choose to sleep either in our luxurious dogominiums or in our Meow Lounge or anywhere in our house. With love and with pampering, they soon feel at home.

We have provided "bed and breakfast" for canine and feline guests for over twenty years, and have never had a problem—mind you, once in a while, the owners are a little hard to handle!

Lilo and Bernie Garich
Countryside Animal Inn, Bonfield, Ontario

HOW'S YOUR DOG, MIKE?

I DUNNO. WE HAD TO LEAVE HIM AT THE VET'S.

WHAT DID HE DO — GET INTO A FIGHT OR SOMETHING?

HE NEVER FIGHTS! FARLEY WOULDN'T HURT A FLEA!

...HE JUST COLLECTS THEM.

DON'T WORRY, MICHAEL. I'M SURE FARLEY WILL BE JUST FINE.

CAN I SAY SOME PRAYERS FOR HIM?

THAT WOULD BE A NICE IDEA.

CAN I GO DIRECTLY TO GOD? — OR DO I ASK FOR SOMEONE IN THE PET DEPARTMENT?

REALLY? — YES, HE DID GET LOOSE FOR A WHILE THE OTHER DAY....

THAT WAS THE VET — FARLEY'S GOING TO BE FINE! — HE JUST ATE SOMETHING THAT MADE HIM SICK.

THERE'S EVEN A NAME FOR IT — "GARBAGE GASTRITIS"...

— AND I WANT NO JOKES ABOUT MY COOKING!!

HE'S A LITTLE SLOW, JUST YET—BUT HE'S FEELING FINE!

HOW CAN WE MAKE SURE HE DOESN'T GET SICK LIKE THIS AGAIN?

WELL, YOU CAN EITHER KEEP HIM IN YOUR OWN BACK YARD, MRS. PATTERSON...

—OR ASK YOUR NEIGHBORS TO PUT OUT BETTER QUALITY GARBAGE.

PTOO

FAR

NOBODY'S PLAYING WIF ME.

EVERYBODY'S PLAYING WIF FARLEY. THEY KEEP HUGGING HIM AN' TALKING TO HIM....

JUST 'CAUSE HE WAS SICK. THAT'S WHY EVERYBODY LIKES HIM BEST.

....DADDY? —I DON'T FEEL WELL.

41

The Party Animal

I remember once, while working a Saturday night at a veterinary emergency clinic, receiving a frantic phone call from a man deeply concerned about his half-grown labrador pup.

"My dog," he wailed, "just gobbled the entire contents of a tray of canapés that I put on the coffee table for my staff Christmas party. What should I do?!"

Puzzled and a little amused, I said, "Well, that's certainly a nuisance for you and your guests. But unless the contents were very spicy, I can't see that they should do the pup much harm. What did the canapés have in them that concerns you so much?"

"Toothpicks!" retorted my caller. "Those little fancy toothpicks with the curly plastic bits at the end. He must have swallowed a dozen of them along with the canapés!"

"If you think you could get him to eat anything else now, here's what I want you to do. Take some soft dog food and mix it up well with several cotton balls and a couple of tablespoons of mineral oil. If you can get that down him, it might do the trick."

I sensed his hesitation but I went on. "The cotton should tangle up the points of the toothpicks and keep them from poking into the gut walls, and the mineral oil will help slide the whole mess through. Give it a try, and let me know how he makes out. If he starts showing any signs of acute pain or fever though, get him down here right away."

It was late the next evening when I recognized the lab's owner on the phone

again. "Just thought I'd let you know that your crazy prescription worked like a charm! They all emerged in one big tangled mass of colored plastic and cotton strands. The dog never showed the slightest sign of discomfort until the moment when he actually passed them. Then you never saw such a puzzled pup in your whole life!"

Beth Cruikshank, D.V.M.,
Miami, Manitoba

MICHAEL- GET GOING BEFORE YOU MISS THAT BUS !!

I'LL TAKE LIZ TO PLAY-CARE, ELLY - AND I'LL LEAVE YOU MY CAR.

AAAH... AN EMPTY HOUSE! - THERE'S NOTHING LIKE AN EMPTY HOUSE — IS THERE, FARLEY.

SIGH...

I don't like to go where my dog can't come with me.

Terri-Lynette Jessup
(age 8),
Crystal River, Fla.

LICK! SLURP-LICK

OOH! UGH!

CUT IT OUT, FARLEY - STOP LICKING ME!

YOU'VE BEEN AWAY SO LONG - HE'S JUST HAPPY TO SEE YOU!

YEAH! MAYBE HE FORGOTS WHAT FLAVOR YOU ARE!

48

LOOK OUT, LIZZIE, WE'RE TRYIN' TO DO THE MOONWALK!

MAAAH! LIZZIE KEEPS HANGIN' 'ROUND WHILE WE'RE TRYING TO DO STUFF!!

ELIZABETH, GO FIND SOMEONE YOUR OWN AGE!

WANNA PLAY TAG?

FARLEY WON'T EAT HIS SUPPER AGAIN, MOM. HE WANTS PEOPLE FOOD!

NO, MICHAEL. IF YOU LET HIM HAVE WHAT WE'RE EATING ALL THE TIME, HE'LL GET SPOILED.

ON THIS STUFF?

WHASSAT? SHHH.... I SNUCK FARLEY A WEENIE OUTA THE FRIDGE!

I'M TELLING! **MOOOM!** YOU SAID NOT TO FEED THE DOG, AN' MICHAEL JUST GIVED HIM A WEEENIE!!

YOU'RE A FINK, ELIZABETH. A DIRTY RAT FINK!

...JUST DOING MY JOB!

 JOHN, FARLEY WAS PICKED UP BY SOMEONE IN A BLUE VAN! A MAN IN THE NEXT BLOCK TOLD ME!

 BLUE VAN?! WHO IN THE WORLD WOULD WANT TO PICK UP FARLEY?

 HERE WE GO, TIM. NO LICENSE, NO COLLAR, NO NOTHING!

 YES, MA'AM... I THINK WE MIGHT HAVE YOUR DOG HERE.

 BIG, SHAGGY... ANSWERS TO "FARLEY", DOES HE.

 SURE, SURE. YOU CAN COME AND PICK HIM UP.

 ....BAIL IS POSTED AT 20 BUCKS.

 THE CHARGE IS: RUNNING AT LARGE — AND WITHOUT A LICENSE.

 YOU'RE LUCKY. THE CHAP WHO CALLED US WANTED TO INCLUDE WILLFUL DAMAGE TO PRIVATE PROPERTY.

 WHAT? WHICH ONE OF OUR NEIGHBORS WOULD TURN IN FARLEY?!

 CHECK THE ONE WITH THE SNOW SCULPTURE.

EASTGATE ANIMAL POUND

For Better or For Worse
By Lynn Johnston

GIGGLE
GIGGLE
GIGGLE

WHAT'S SO FUNNY?

YOU PUT (GIGGLE) YOUR UNDERWEAR OUT ON THE CLOTHES LINE!
GIGGLE GIGGLE

WHAT'S SO FUNNY ABOUT THAT?

HONESTLY, MICHAEL, IN THIS DAY AND AGE, I CAN HARDLY SEE HOW A FEW UNDER-CLOTHES COULD....

HA HA! HAHA HAHAHA HAH! HA HAHAH HA! HA HA HA HA!! GIGGLE HAAH!

Animals can be noble creatures, ones that can teach us how to value joy and sorrow. They make an important contribution to all of our struggles to become or remain compassionate.

Okey Goode, Clarkson, Wash.

59

60

DADDY, I CAN'T MAKE FARLEY DO ANYTHING. HE WON'T SIT, HE WON'T LIE DOWN — HE'S A DUMB DOG!

HE'S NOT A DUMB DOG, ELIZABETH. YOU HAVE TO HAVE AUTHORITY IN YOUR VOICE. YOU MAKE A STRONG, SIMPLE COMMAND — LIKE THIS:

FARLEY? SIT!!

DUMB DOG.

NOW, KEEPING THE DOG AT THE END OF A LONG LEAD... GIVE THE COMMAND TO "COME"!

IMMEDIATELY, PULL HIM TOWARD YOU. WITH REPETITION, HIS RESPONSE TO THE WORD "COME" WILL BE AUTOMATIC.

COULD YOU COME DOWN HERE, MIKE? .... MIKE?! —MICHAEL?!!!

GOT ANOTHER ONE OF THOSE LEADS?

I'VE DONE IT, EL. FARLEY NOW OBEYS 4 COMMANDS PERFECTLY!

IT'S TAKEN PATIENCE AND PERSEVERANCE, BUT MY LITTLE OBEDIENCE PROGRAM IS A SUCCESS.

OWOOOOOOOOooooo

DADDY... YOUR SUCCESS IS HOWLING.

66

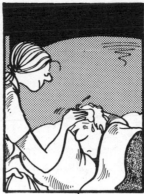

I DON'T MEAN TO COMPLAIN, HON, BUT THE LAST TIME YOU DID THAT, THE CLOTH SMELLED FUNNY.

HONEY, HAVE YOU NOTICED THAT THE DOG IS LIMPING?

I WONDER WHAT IT IS THAT MAKES HIM WALK LIKE THAT?

SHOULD WE HAVE HIM CHECKED? MAYBE THERE'S SOMETHING WRONG!

YAH! MAYBE HE GOTS ARFRITIS!!

NO WONDER THE DOG'S LIMPING. LOOK AT ALL THE STUFF STUCK TO THE HAIR BETWEEN HIS TOES!

WE'LL HAVE TO DO SOMETHING TO KEEP HIM FROM PICKING UP ALL THAT DIRT AND SNOW.

For Better or For Worse
By Lynn Johnston

79

*E*very Christmas we give our lab, Shorty, a treat. We gift wrap it and put it under the tree. She knows which one is hers, but she always waits until we're all seated and opening our gifts before she opens hers!

Kieran Donnelly, Sydney N.S.W.

80

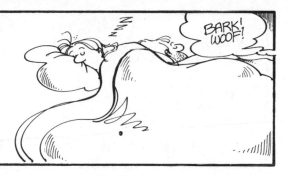

For Better or For Worse

By Lynn Johnston

BLEAH!

DOG

SCRAPE SCRAPE SCRAPE

THAT'S THE SECOND BOWL OF DOG FOOD I'VE THROWN OUT THIS WEEK. THIS DOG WON'T EAT A THING!!

YAWN

SURE HE WILL. HE JUST WANTS TO EAT WHAT WE'RE EATING.

IF HE KNOWS WHAT YOU'RE PUTTING OUT IS FOR DOGS, HE'S NOT INTERESTED....

BUT IF HE THINKS IT'S PEOPLE FOOD, HE'LL EAT ANYTHING YOU PUT IN FRONT OF HIM!

GOURMET DOG FOOD

HERE.

SPLOIP!

.... MAKE IT LOOK GOOD.

OK, WE GOT THE SPIDER OUT OF THE MICROWAVE. WHERE DO YOU WANT US TO PUT IT?

OUTSIDE.

WHAT YOU WERE ABOUT TO DO WAS CRUEL AND HORRIBLE! HE HAS AS MUCH RIGHT TO LIVE AS YOU DO!

....SET HIM FREE!!

"CHOMP"!!

OK, GUYS! I'M CONVINCED. I'M NOT GOING TO MY MEETING TONIGHT. I'M STAYING HOME WITH YOU! HAPPY?

UH HUH.

WELL— SHOULD WE PLAY MONOPOLY? SCRABBLE? DO SOME BAKING TOGETHER? WHAT WOULD YOU LIKE TO DO?

NOTHIN'

NOTHING?!! THEN WHY DID YOU WANT ME TO STAY HOME?

I DUNNO... I GUESS IT'S SORTA LIKE OWNING A DOG.

...YOU DON'T ALWAYS WANNA DO SOMETHING WITH THEM, BUT IT'S SURE GREAT HAVING THEM AROUND!!

I AM STARVING, AND THERE'S NOTHING GOOD TO EAT AROUND HERE!! NO CANDY, NO CAKE— NO NOTHING!!

WOULD A WOGGIE LIKE A COOKIE? COOKIE FOR A WOGGER? HE WANTS A NUM-NUM? YES HE DOES!!

SHAKE SHAKE SHAKE

TASTELESS.... BUT EDIBLE.

MUNCH GRUNCH

WHO DO YOU LIKE BEST, MOM? ME OR MICHAEL?

I LIKE YOU BOTH.

I MEAN, WHO'S EASIER TO BRING UP? ME OR HIM?

YOU ARE BOTH EQUALLY CHALLENGING.

BUT WHICH ONE OF US IN THIS FAMILY DOES WHAT THEY'RE TOLD THE MOST, IS GOOD THE MOST, AN' IS MOST EASIEST TO LIVE WITH?

....SHE CHOSE THE DOG.

IT'S SO FRESH AND BRIGHT OUT THERE, AND HERE WE ARE WORKING IN A STUFFY HOUSE!

WHY DON'T YOU OPEN THE DOOR, EL, AND LET SOME OF THIS BEAUTIFUL DAY INSIDE!

SOMETHING'S THE MATTER WITH THE DOG, MOM. HE KEEPS LICKING AT A SPOT ON HIS LEG.

IT LOOKS LIKE A DEEP CUT! I WONDER HOW THAT HAPPENED!

GET SOME WARM WATER, SOME ANTISEPTIC AND THE SCISSORS. I'LL HAVE TO CUT AWAY SOME OF HIS FUR.

KNOW WHAT, MOM? YOU'RE THE BEST MOTHER A DOG COULD HAVE!!

FARLEY'S REALLY LIMPING, MOM, AN' HE'S CHEWED THROUGH THE BANDAGE YOU PUT ON HIM. ...SHOULD WE TAKE HIM TO THE VET?

I DON'T THINK SO. THE WOUND'S NOT INFECTED. ...BUT I WONDER WHY IT WON'T HEAL!

WHAT DO YOU SAY, FARL? SHOULD WE LEAVE IT FOR ANOTHER DAY AND SEE WHAT HAPPENS?

...SOMETIMES I WISH HE WASN'T SO TRUSTING!!

LICK!

110

I SUPPOSE I'M SITTING ON YOUR END OF THE COUCH.

LET ME TELL YOU SOMETHING, FARL. ...I OWN THIS COUCH, SEE.

I OWN THIS COUCH, AND I GOT HERE FIRST. IF I'M SITTING IN YOUR SPOT, THAT'S JUST TOO DARNED BAD.

I'M NOT MOVING, SO YOU'LL JUST HAVE TO COMPROMISE.

YOU LIKE ME, DON'T YOU, FARLEY. YOU LIKE ME NO MATTER WHAT.

DOGS DON'T CARE WHO YOU ARE, OR HOW YOU LOOK... THEY LOVE YOU ANYWAY.

DOGS WERE MADE TO MAKE YOU HAPPY.

.... I WONDER WHY GOD LET **PEOPLE** RUN THE WORLD.

Our dog, Tiger, used to love our lawn sprinkler. He would jump around when we turned it on, and then try to bite the spray. He also loved to swim!

One of the things I remember most about my childhood is the smell of a happy, wet dog, and the feel of his "kisses" on my cheek.

Taylor Knight, Durham, N.C.

118

We loved our puppy for sixteen years, ever since she was found covered with tar, wandering around a relative's farm down in West Virginia. She was six years old when our daughter, Cheryl, was born, so Mandy, like Farley, grew up with babies. She was an important part of our family!

Craig and Diane Menz,
Parma Heights, Ohio

HAH! MICHAEL'S GONE! AT LAST THE WHOLE REC-ROOM IS **MINE**!!

I'VE GOT THE COUCH, THE CHANNEL CHANGER, THE BEST CUSHION, THE DOG AN' THE POPCORN!

THERE'S ONLY ONE THING BETTER THAN HAVING EVERYTHING TO YOURSELF...

... AN' THAT'S HAVING SOMEONE TO SHARE IT WITH.

MOM, DAWN AN' I ARE GOING OVER TO HARRISON'S POND. CAN WE TAKE FARLEY?

I GUESS SO.

IF YOU'RE TAKING YOUR BIKES, WAIT FOR HIM. IT'S A HOT DAY, AND HE CAN'T RUN LIKE HE USED TO.

HE'S 9 NOW. HE'S GETTING TO BE AN OLD DOG. DOGS AGE JUST LIKE PEOPLE DO!

YOU MEAN, IF YOU SHAVED OFF HIS FACE, HE'D HAVE WRINKLES?

I LOVE HARRISON'S POND! - DON'T YOU, LIZ?

YEAH!

— YOU NEVER KNOW WHAT KINDS OF GROSS, DISGUSTING THINGS YOU'LL FIND IN IT!!

I will give Samantha, my thirteen-year-old
shepherd-collie, an extra hug every day that
I can for the remaining time that I'm lucky
enough to have her.

Jo Ann H., Dayton, Ohio

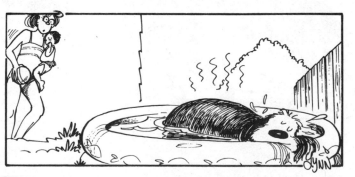

For Better or For Worse
By Lynn Johnston

MY MOTHER ONCE TOLD ME THAT SOMEDAY, I'D BE PUT ON A PEDESTAL.

THAT A MAN WOULD BE SO DEVOTED TO ME, HE'D WORSHIP THE GROUND I WALKED ON... HE'D FOLLOW ME ABOUT...

THAT HE'D LOVE AND ADORE ME WITHOUT QUESTION — AND WHAT DID I GET?

....A SHORT, HAIRY, OVERWEIGHT GUY, WITH BAD BREATH AND A POOR VOCABULARY.

Lynn

FARLEY'S A LITTLE SLOW THESE DAYS, JOHN.

MAYBE IT'S THE HEAT.

MAYBE HE MISSES MICHAEL. HE'S NEVER BEEN AWAY FROM HOME THIS LONG BEFORE.

THERE'S A SORT OF EMPTY FEELING AROUND HERE.

WHEN YOU GO INTO HIS ROOM, IT SEEMS SO STRANGE, SOMEHOW.

YEAH.

... MAYBE WE SHOULDN'T HAVE TIDIED IT.

Lynn

SNIFFF WHUFFA SNURFF SNUFF SNIFF

ERK?

GAH!

?

HEY, MOM!! APRIL SAT UP ALL BY HERSELF!!

Lynn

132

For Better or For Worse
By Lynn Johnston

138

For Better or For Worse

By Lynn Johnston

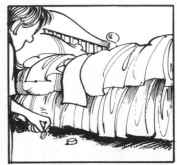

For Better or For Worse

By Lynn Johnston

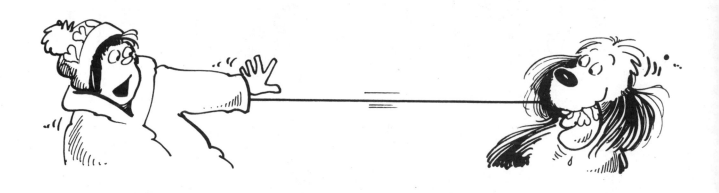

149

For Better or For Worse

By Lynn Johnston

GOOD. I SEE MIKE BATHED THE DOG LIKE I ASKED HIM TO !!

For Better or For Worse

By Lynn Johnston

FLAP
FLAP

MHHHHHH

SOMEDAY, EL, I'M GOING TO HAVE MY CAR TO MYSELF. I WILL CLIMB INTO IT, AND THE TANK WILL SAY "FULL".

SOMEDAY, WE'LL HAVE THE HOUSE TO OUR-SELVES. THE ROOMS WILL STAY TIDY, THE FLOORS WILL STAY CLEAN.

SOMEDAY...

DADDY? ...WANT HUGGY?

...AND I HOPE IT DOESN'T COME TOO SOON.

I-GEEN?

I-GEEN!

I GOT I-GEEN!!!

I-GEEN AW-GONE!

CRUNSCH MFF SCH GRUNCH

MMMFF!

SLUPP SLORP! SLURP SLURP SLORP SLOORP

156

For Better or For Worse
By Lynn Johnston

160

THERE'S ONE THING I HATE ABOUT REALLY COLD DAYS....

EVERY TIME I GO INTO THE HOUSE...

....MY GLASSES FOG UP.

DON'T SLEEP IN THE DOORWAY, FARLEY! EVERYONE TRIPS OVER YOU!—COME HERE, BOY!

FARLEY! FARLEY?—WHAT'S THE MATTER? WHY DON'T YOU COME WHEN I CALL YOU?

CAN'T YOU HEAR ME?

YOU **CAN** HEAR ME... CAN'T YOU?

MOM, I DON'T THINK FARLEY HEARS VERY WELL.

I KNOW, HONEY.

I TOOK HIM TO THE VET LAST WEEK. THE DOCTOR TOLD ME THAT HE DOESN'T SEE TOO WELL NOW, EITHER.

FARLEY IS OVER 80 IN OUR YEARS. THESE THINGS HAPPEN WHEN YOU GET OLDER.—PETS ARE JUST LIKE PEOPLE!

...EXCEPT THAT THEY NEVER COMPLAIN!!

*O*ne of the happy memories of my childhood is of George, the post office dog, an old yellow dog who slept in front of the old post office door, and whose portrait hangs in the "new" Manhattan Beach post office still. As a bum, in his youth, he'd stopped a robbery at the post office. He was a local hero. When I was a child, he was an old dog, and an old dog treated with great respect, his story told to every new person who stepped over him to enter.

Then there's my old cat Milo, who was gone for two years and showed up at another house when I moved there. These things are a part of my heart and a part of what gives me enthusiasm for life, a faith in grace.

Alison McMahon, Angelus Oaks, Calif.

SERA WON'T BE TOO FAR AWAY, CONNIE. SHE KNOWS HER WAY AROUND HERE.

SERAAAAHHH

THAT'S NOT THE POINT, EL. SHE JUST SHOULDN'T BE RUNNING AROUND LOOSE RIGHT NOW!

OH. I SEE.

WE HAVE TO FIND HER BEFORE, YOU KNOW... SOMETHING HAPPENS! I MEAN, WHAT IF SHE MEETS SOME UGLY, STUPID NEIGHBORHOOD......

...MUTT.

SAY YOU'RE SORRY, APRIL.

INE SOWWY.

SHE DIDN'T KNOW THAT SERA WASN'T SUPPOSED TO BE LOOSE, CONNIE.

OH WELL. I GUESS IT'S TOO LATE NOW.

WE NEVER REALLY SAW THEM, CONNIE! HOW CAN YOU BE SO SURE THAT SOMETHING...... HAPPENED?

BECAUSE, THIS IS THE FIRST TIME I'VE ACTUALLY SEEN A DOG SMILE.

SO, IS FARLEY GOING TO BE SLAPPED WITH A PATERNITY SUIT?

DON'T JOKE ABOUT THIS, JOHN... IT'S SERIOUS!

YOU CAN SAY "BOYS WILL BE BOYS," AND YOU CAN TALK ABOUT "SOWING WILD OATS," BUT HE'S OURS, AND WHAT HE DOES IS OUR RESPONSIBILITY!

...LEAVE HIM ALONE FOR ONE MINUTE, AND ∗TSK∗ - IF IT'S NOT ONE THING, IT'S ANOTHER!

THAT REMINDS ME... HAS ANYONE HEARD FROM MICHAEL?

166

WELL, IT'S A FACT, EL. SERA'S GOING TO HAVE PUPS, AND SHE'S DUE AROUND THE FIRST WEEK OF NOVEMBER.

DID YOU HEAR THAT, FARLEY? WE'RE HOLDING YOU RESPONSIBLE!

GOSH, CONNIE. I REALLY DON'T KNOW WHAT TO SAY. - I HOPE YOU'RE NOT ANGRY.

ANGRY?!!

ELLY, I'M GOING TO BE A GRANDMA!!

SERA'S GOING TO HAVE PUPPIES? OH, MAN! THAT IS SO COOL!!!

CAN WE GET ONE, MOM? IF FARLEY'S THE DADDY, WE SHOULD GET ONE!!

I DON'T THINK SO, ELIZABETH.

YOU'RE NOT GONNA LET CONNIE GIVE THEM AWAY, ARE YOU? YOU WOULDN'T LET HER GIVE THEM AWAY!!!

YEAH, EL...

AFTER ALL - THEY'RE YOUR GRANDPUPPIES, TOO!!

GUESS WHAT, DAD! SERA'S GONNA HAVE PUPS - AN' WE MIGHT GET ONE!

I SAID WE'D THINK ABOUT IT! I NEVER SAID FOR SURE. I JUST SAID WE'D THINK ABOUT IT! - AND THERE'S PLENTY OF TIME TO MAKE A DECISION!

I MUST CAUTION YOU, ELIZABETH. WE REALLY DON'T WANT ANOTHER DOG, SO PLEASE... DON'T GET YOUR HOPES UP.

YESS!!

167

MOM, MOM! THE PUPPIES ARE HERE! SERA HAD HER PUPPIES!!!

OH, CONNIE — THEY'RE ADORABLE!

SHE HAD THEM EARLY THIS MORNING.

LOOKIT HOW LITTLE THEY ARE! WHY ARE NEW-BORNED BABIES SO TEENY-TINY?

TRUST ME, APRIL...IT'S EASIER THAT WAY.

169

For Better or For Worse

By Lynn Johnston

181

183

ELLY, WHY DON'T YOU AND MOM TAKE APRIL UP TO THE HOUSE AND GET WARM...I'LL BE THERE IN A MINUTE.

DADDY....

HEY, FARLEY! WHAT'S THE MATTER, OLD BOY? WHAT'S THE MATTER?!!

DADDY.....HE ISN'T BREATHING!!

I WENT BACK DOWN TO THE RIVER, AND I WRAPPED HIM IN A BLANKET.

ELIZABETH AND I PUT HIM IN THE CAR, AND DROVE INTO TOWN.

THE VETERINARIAN SAID IT WAS HIS HEART. HE SAID THAT THE COLD AND THE STRESS WERE TOO MUCH FOR HIM.

FARLEY WAS AN OLD DOG, JOHN.

I KNOW.

...BUT I DIDN'T THINK THAT A HEART SO BIG WOULD EVER STOP BEATING.

IT'S A BEAUTIFUL NIGHT TONIGHT, ISN'T IT, GRANDMA.

IT IS INDEED.-JUST LOOK AT ALL THOSE STARS.

SOME NIGHTS THEY SEEM TO BE BRIGHTER THAN OTHER NIGHTS. SOME NIGHTS, IT FEELS AS THOUGH YOU COULD REACH OUT AND TOUCH ONE!

YOU CAN'T REALLY TOUCH A STAR, CAN YOU, GRANDMA?

OH, I THINK I COULD TOUCH ONE TONIGHT, APRIL.

IN FACT... I COULD HUG TWO OF THEM!!

184

*T*his (story) held special meaning for me, in that a month ago I took our dog and stayed with him as the veterinarian put him to sleep. I stayed because he always came to where I was, and was always waiting when I would come home. I have enclosed a poem I wrote at the time. Now retired and in my 60s, I am finally trying to get serious about writing poetry. This is the first one I have had the nerve to share.

A Friendship

We met late in life,
both in our sixties.
It was not an immediate liking.
It took us a time
to become friends.
Each had habits
that annoyed the other.
I thought him demanding,
interrupting me no matter
how I was engaged.
He must of thought me indifferent
when I ignored him
and went about my way.
These differences were overgrown
by the friendship we came to share.

The passing years weighed
on both of us.
We did less, but were
together more.
Sleep crept increasingly into his day.
He had difficulty getting up,
and needed help with stairs.
One night he fell out of bed,
and laid despairingly on the floor.
In the morning I put him
in the car, then sat with him
in the waiting room until
another hand
took his leash.

March 16, 1995
Sterling P.C. Hum
Sherman Oaks, Calif.

*F*arley died loved and belonging to us all. And his death was not a senseless event. The day my dog, Sass, died a few years back, I saved another cartoon with another dog—Snoopy—being encouraged by Lucy to write something profound and thought-provoking. He wrote: "Are there dogs in Heaven?" Yes! Yes! And yes again! They'll certainly be there in all the memories that each of us carries.

Charlene Fairchild,
Springfield, Ontario

THE CONSERVATION AUTHOR-ITIES ALLOWED US TO BURY FARLEY HERE IN THE RAVINE.

IT'S A LOVELY SPOT, DEAR.

MOM'S GOING TO PLANT SOME FLOWERS SO WE KNOW WHERE HE IS.

WHAT A FINE IDEA! ... I WONDER WHAT KIND!

I'M NOT SURE BUT I THINK IT'S "REINCARNATIONS".

There is tremendous personal significance in the death of a treasured pet. As we experience this passage with them, we wonder how much they understand. Their gentle and uncomplaining acceptance of age suggests that they are much more aware of what lies beyond this mortal life than we are.

I miss my Anna terribly. She was a mutt. We were together for fifteen years. Still, something tells me that we'll be together again. It won't be heaven unless she's there to meet me!

Lorraine Chan,
Los Angeles,
Calif.

For Better or For Worse

By Lynn Johnston

IS THIS THE PLACE?

UH HUH.

I'M REALLY SORRY, LIZ.

THANKS. ME TOO.

I'M GLAD THEY LET US BURY HIM HERE. WE'RE GOING TO CALL THIS FARLEY'S TREE. WHEN IT'S WARM ENOUGH.... WE'RE GOING TO PLANT SOME FLOWERS.

NICE.

I DIDN'T THINK I'D MISS HIM LIKE THIS, DAWN. I NEVER THOUGHT THAT A DOG COULD MEAN SO MUCH.

I KNOW.

SOMETIMES, I THINK I'LL SEE HIM AGAIN. I TRY TO IMAGINE WHAT HEAVEN IS LIKE... WHAT IT'S LIKE TO BE THERE.

DO YOU BELIEVE IN GHOSTS, ELIZABETH?

NOT REALLY.

BUT IT'S STRANGE ...AND PROBABLY MY IMAGINATION..

WHAT?

... SOMETIMES, I HEAR THE SOUND OF HIS COLLAR....AS IF HE WAS WALKING RIGHT HERE.

HI! — HI... WHEN YOU WEREN'T AT THE HOUSE, I THOUGHT I'D FIND YOU HERE.

THIS IS FARLEY'S TREE, ISN'T IT. — YEAH. I LIKE TO COME HERE WHEN I NEED TO THINK.

YOU THINK ABOUT HIM A LOT, DON'T YOU. — WE ALL DO... ESPECIALLY MOM. I THINK HE WAS MORE HER DOG THAN ANYONE'S.

THE LITTLE FLOWERS SHE PLANTED ARE PRETTY! WHAT ARE THEY? — FORGET-ME-NOTS.

WHAT'S BOTHERING YOU, MIKE? — I CAN'T WRITE.

FOR THE PAST 2 DAYS I'VE BEEN TRYING TO DO A NEWSPAPER ARTICLE -YOU KNOW, LOCAL INTEREST STUFF- BUT NOTHING I'VE THOUGHT OF WORKS!!

MAYBE I'M HEADING IN THE WRONG DIRECTION. MAYBE I'M TOO EMOTIONAL FOR THIS! I'M FULL OF SELF-DOUBT, I'M SARCASTIC AND COMPULSIVE AND ANALYTICAL... AND, HALF THE TIME, I LIVE IN A FANTASY WORLD!!

... I DON'T HAVE ANY OF THE CREATIVE ELEMENTS THAT MAKE SOMEONE A **WRITER!**

IS THIS WHERE IT HAPPENED? — YES. APRIL FELL INTO THE RIVER RIGHT HERE.

SHE STILL HAS BAD DREAMS ABOUT IT. SHE STILL THINKS IT'S HER FAULT THAT FARLEY DIED -BUT SHE'S GETTING BETTER.

WHY DON'T YOU WRITE ABOUT IT? WHY DON'T YOU WRITE ABOUT WHAT HAPPENED THAT DAY? — BECAUSE, IT WOULD BE LIKE HAVING MAJOR SURGERY.

MIKE, ONE HAS SURGERY WHEN SOMETHING NEEDS TO COME OUT.

*I*t is with grateful thanks that I acknowledge all of the fine people who have written to me over the years, sharing their thoughts, anecdotes, and deep, personal feelings.

I appreciate your wisdom, your wit, and your thoughtfulness, especially in response to "Farley."

Sincerely,

Lynn Johnston